Unhurried

A Devotional Journey into God's Rest

By Ruth Conlon

Eternal *life*
Publishers

EternalLife Publishers is a publishing ministry with a passion for spiritual development. We produce individual and group resources to accompany you on your sacred journey. For more information on our training and products, go to www.pursuingholiness.org. EternalLife Publishers is the publishing arm of Pursuing Holiness Ministries.

Email: info@pursuingholiness.org

Published by EternalLife Publishers, a part of Pursuing Holiness Ministries

London, England

www.pursuingholiness.org

Book Layout by EternalLife Publishers

Cover designed by EternalLife Publishers

All Scripture quotations are taken from the New King James Version® (unless otherwise stated). Copyright © 1982 by Thomas Nelson. Used by permission. All rights reserved.

Unhurried / Ruth Conlon. –1st Ed.

ISBN 978-0-9934696-5-7

Table of Contents

Introduction

There's a quiet invitation echoing beneath the noise of our lives.

It's not loud or urgent. It doesn't compete with deadlines or demand attention. But if you still yourself long enough, you'll hear it. It's the voice of the Shepherd whispering, "Come away with Me. Let Me give rest to your soul."

We live in a world that rushes — always reaching, always running, always restless. And in that constant motion, something sacred is lost: stillness. Presence. Peace. We forget how to be. We forget how to breathe. We forget how to dwell with God.

This devotional is an invitation to remember.

Unhurried is not just a pace. It's a posture of heart. It's a way of being with God that allows His Spirit to move freely, deeply, slowly — shaping us from the inside out. It's not lazy, passive, or indifferent. Rather, it is deliberate, attentive, and surrendered. This is the sacred slow.

These 100 devotions are written to guide you on a journey of rest and renewal. They are best used on a personal retreat or in quiet moments set aside from the busyness of daily life. You may choose to read one a day, or linger on a few over the course of a weekend. There is no hurry here.

Each devotional includes:

- A **Scripture** to center your heart

- A **Reflection** to awaken your soul

- A **Prayer** to guide your conversation with God

- And occasionally, a **Prompt** to stir journaling or silence

Let this be a journey of presence over performance, abiding over achieving, stillness over striving. May the God who is never in a rush meet you in every word. May you rediscover the beauty of walking with Him at His pace.

The unhurried life isn't a luxury – it's a necessity for the soul. And God is waiting, not at the finish line, but here, in the quiet.

You don't have to run anymore.

You don't have to prove anything.

You don't have to hold it all together.

You just have to come.

And rest.

1

The God Who Walks Slowly

Scripture

Genesis 3:8 - "Then the man and his wife heard the sound of the Lord God as he was walking in the garden in the cool of the day..." (NIV)

Reflection

God doesn't rush through gardens. He walks. Step by step. Slow. Present.

From the very beginning, we see a God who moves at a pace that invites relationship—not performance. In Eden, God walked with Adam and Eve. It was unhurried, unforced, and full of presence.

Even after the Fall, He still came walking—seeking. And that's the same way He comes to you today.

We often expect God to run into our chaos and fix everything. But more often, He invites us to slow down and walk with Him instead. The unhurried life begins by matching our steps with His.

Prayer

Lord, teach me to walk with You in the cool of the day. Slow me down. Quiet my soul. Help me to feel Your presence with every step.

Prompt

What pace have you been walking at lately? Take a walk with God today, intentionally slow, and invite Him to speak as you go.

2

The Pace of Eden

Scripture

Psalm 23:2 - "He makes me lie down in green pastures, he leads me beside quiet waters…" (NIV)

Reflection

Eden was a place of peace, abundance, and stillness. No striving. No deadlines. No rush.

We were created to live in rhythm with the Creator—resting, walking, working, and worshiping in harmony with Him.

But we've traded the green pastures for glowing screens and endless lists. God is calling us back to Eden—not a place, but a posture. A life led beside still waters, nourished in His presence.

When God leads, it is never at a pace that burns you out. If you're exhausted, it might be time to check who's setting the pace.

Prayer

Shepherd of my soul, lead me back to the still waters. Let me lie down in the green pastures of Your peace. Restore what hurry has drained from me.

Prompt

Find a quiet space today—no phone, no noise. Imagine Eden. Ask God what still waters look like for your life right now.

3
The Hurry Within

Scripture
Isaiah 30:15 - "In repentance and rest is your salvation, in quietness and trust is your strength..." (NIV)

Reflection
Hurry is not just external—it's internal. A restless soul, a mind that won't quiet, a heart always striving.

The Israelites were told their strength would be found in rest and quiet, but they refused. We often do the same. We think hustle is holiness and busyness equals value.

But God doesn't measure us by pace. He meets us in stillness. When we slow down, we realise that peace was available all along—just beneath the surface of our striving.

Silence is strength. Repentance is rest. Trust is enough.

Prayer
Father, I repent of the hurry I've carried. Quiet the noise within me. Teach me to trust that You are enough, even when I'm not doing anything at all.

Prompt
Set a timer for five minutes. Sit in silence. Breathe deeply. When your mind wanders, gently bring it back to God's presence.

Rest is Resistance

Scripture

Exodus 20:8-10 - "Remember the Sabbath day by keeping it holy. Six days you shall labour and do all your work, but the seventh day is a sabbath to the Lord your God." (NIV)

Reflection

Rest is not just a gift—it's a declaration of trust. When we rest, we proclaim that God is God and we are not. We lay down our need to prove, to perform, to produce.

In a world driven by constant output, Sabbath is resistance. It is a holy rebellion against the systems that tell us our worth is in our work.

God gave Sabbath to free us, not to burden us. He wanted His people to taste Eden again. To rest is to remember we belong to Him—not to Pharaoh, not to culture, not even to our own ambitions.

Prayer

Lord of the Sabbath, help me resist the pull to find my value in doing. Teach me to rest as an act of worship and freedom.

Prompt

How can you incorporate a regular rhythm of rest that reflects trust in God? What would a Sabbath day look like for your soul?

5

Time as Gift, Not Master

Scripture

Ecclesiastes 3:1 - "There is a time for everything, and a season for every activity under the heavens." (NIV)

Reflection

Time is not your enemy. It's not running out. It's not working against you. Time is a gift from the One who holds all things.

We often live like time is our master—chasing it, fearing it, regretting it. But God gave time so we could learn rhythm, trust, and surrender.

When you surrender to God's timing, you move from anxiety to peace. From control to contentment. You learn to live within the sacred now.

Prayer

Eternal God, help me to see time as Your gift. Teach me to live in step with Your seasons and not be ruled by fear or hurry.

Prompt

Reflect on your relationship with time. Do you feel ruled by the clock? Ask God to help you see time as a space to receive, not just to achieve.

6

Sacred Interruptions

Scripture

Luke 8:44-46 - "She came up behind him and touched the edge of his cloak… But Jesus said, 'Someone touched me; I know that power has gone out from me.'" (NIV)

Reflection

Jesus was never too busy to be interrupted. While on His way to heal a dying child, He stopped for a woman with an issue of blood. She wasn't part of His public itinerary, but she was seen.

The unhurried life welcomes interruption—not as inconvenience, but as invitation. Some of the most sacred encounters come in the unexpected moments we didn't plan.

When we slow down, we begin to see people again. We hear their pain. We feel their touch. And we respond like Christ—present, gentle, full of power.

Prayer

Jesus, help me not to miss the sacred interruptions. Slow my steps so I can see who You are putting in my path today.

Prompt

Think about your last interruption. How did you respond? Ask God to help you see such moments through His eyes.

7

The Slow Work of God

Scripture

Philippians 1:6 – "Being confident of this, that he who began a good work in you will carry it on to completion until the day of Christ Jesus." (NIV)

Reflection

God works in seasons, not seconds. His transforming grace is often gentle, layered, and deep.

We grow frustrated when change feels slow, but God is more interested in lasting fruit than quick fixes. His work in us is deliberate and patient.

Trust the slow work of God. The roots are going deep even when the surface seems still. He is shaping something eternal in you.

Prayer

God of all time, help me to trust Your pace. Teach me patience in the process, and faith in Your unseen work.

Prompt

Where have you been impatient with your growth? What might God be doing beneath the surface that you cannot yet see?

8

When God Says 'Wait'

Scripture

Psalm 27:14 - "Wait for the Lord; be strong and take heart and wait for the Lord." (NIV)

Reflection

Waiting is not wasted time. It is sacred space where God deepens trust, clarifies vision, and refines character.

When God says "wait," He is not withholding out of cruelty but preparing out of love. The waiting room of God is where endurance is built and intimacy is born.

What feels like a delay may be divine preparation. Stay. Watch. Trust. He is working while you wait.

Prayer

Lord, give me grace to wait well. Help me not to rush ahead or despair in delay. I choose to trust that You are working in the waiting.

Prompt

Write about a time when waiting led to unexpected blessing. How did it shape your trust in God?

9

Slowness is Not Laziness

Scripture

2 Peter 3:9 - "The Lord is not slow in keeping his promise, as some understand slowness. Instead he is patient with you..." (NIV)

Reflection

We confuse speed with value. In a culture that prizes efficiency, slowness can feel like failure.

But God is not in a rush. His slowness is not neglect—it is mercy. His timing is not careless—it is intentional.

To walk slowly through life with God is not to be lazy, but to be present. Purposeful. Aligned with heaven's rhythm. Let others sprint. You've been invited to walk with the King.

Prayer

Patient God, free me from the pressure to rush. Let me not confuse slowness with weakness. Teach me to value what You value.

Prompt

What areas of your life have you tried to speed up? Ask God what it means to walk in His timing instead of your own.

10

The Freedom of Saying No

Scripture

Matthew 5:37 - "All you need to say is simply 'Yes' or 'No'; anything beyond this comes from the evil one." (NIV)

Reflection

Hurry often comes from overcommitment. We say yes too quickly, afraid to disappoint, afraid to miss out, afraid to seem unspiritual.

But Jesus never said yes to everything. He moved with purpose, not pressure. He withdrew often. He knew when to say no.

Saying no is not selfish—it is sacred. It protects the space God needs to move in your life. Let your no be a holy act of trust.

Prayer

Lord, give me wisdom to know what to say yes to and courage to say no when needed. Help me honour Your pace, not people's expectations.

Prompt

Are there any commitments or pressures in your life that need a prayerful no? Take time to ask God where He wants you to create space.

11

Breath as Prayer

Scripture

Job 33:4 - "The Spirit of God has made me; the breath of the Almighty gives me life." (NIV)

Reflection

Sometimes prayer is not words—it's breath. Inhale His presence. Exhale your fear. Inhale His peace. Exhale your striving.

Your breath is a gift, a rhythm of life given by the Spirit. In slowing down to breathe, you realign your soul with heaven.

Let each breath be an act of worship. A prayer without words. A reminder that God is near, and you are alive in Him.

Prayer

Breath of Life, fill me afresh. Slow me down. Let my very breath become a prayer that honours You and welcomes Your presence.

Prompt

Pause and take five slow, deep breaths. With each inhale, whisper a name of God. With each exhale, let go of something weighing you down.

12

Sabbath: A Gift We Forgot

Scripture

Mark 2:27 - "Then he said to them, 'The Sabbath was made for man, not man for the Sabbath.'" (NIV)

Reflection

Sabbath is not a rule to keep but a rhythm to receive. It is a gift—a divine pause where we remember that we are loved, not for what we do, but for who we are.

In our effort to be productive, we've forgotten how to rest. And in forgetting rest, we've forgotten trust.

Sabbath reorients our hearts. It reminds us that God is Provider, Sustainer, and Lord. We stop not because we're done, but because He is enough.

Prayer

Lord of rest, restore my love for Sabbath. Help me not to treat it as a burden but to receive it as a gift of grace and joy.

Prompt

Plan a Sabbath day this week. What could it look like to stop, delight, rest, and worship without guilt?

13

The Gentle Voice

Scripture

1 Kings 19:12 - "And after the fire came a gentle whisper." (NIV)

Reflection

Elijah had seen fire and wind and earthquake. But God wasn't in the noise—He was in the whisper.

The hurried heart looks for God in the dramatic. The unhurried heart hears Him in the quiet.

God still speaks in gentle ways. In whispers. In nudges. In silence that stirs the soul. Are you quiet enough to hear Him?

Prayer

Speak, Lord, in the stillness. Quiet every other voice until only Yours remains. Let me recognise Your whisper and respond with joy.

Prompt

Find a silent space today. No music, no words, no agenda. Just listen. Write down what you sense or notice.

14

Learning to Linger

Scripture

Psalm 27:4 - "One thing I ask from the Lord... that I may dwell in the house of the Lord all the days of my life..." (NIV)

Reflection

God doesn't rush us out of His presence. We do that to ourselves.

We're often too busy to linger. But some of the deepest transformation happens not in moving on, but in staying.

To linger is to love. To dwell is to desire. When you stop rushing through time with God, your heart begins to open in new ways.

Prayer

Lord, help me not to treat our time as something to get through. Teach me to dwell with You, to linger in love, and to enjoy being in Your presence.

Prompt

During your time with God today, stay five minutes longer than usual. Notice what changes in your spirit when you do.

15

Slowing Down for Love

Scripture

1 Corinthians 13:4 - "Love is patient…" (NIV)

Reflection

Love never hurries. It makes space. It waits. It listens.

To live unhurried is to live in love. Hurry is often rooted in self—what we need, want, or fear. Love is always others-focused.

Slowing down gives you the ability to truly see others, to respond with compassion, to love as Christ loves.

Let your pace reflect your priorities. If love is the greatest commandment, your life must be slow enough to obey it.

Prayer

God of love, slow me down until my life moves at the pace of love. Let patience rise in me as I choose compassion over speed.

Prompt

Think of one person you often rush past or respond to impatiently. What could it look like to slow down and love them today?

PART TWO:
SURRENDERED AND STILL

16

The Unburdening

Scripture

Matthew 11:28 - "Come to me, all you who are weary and burdened, and I will give you rest." (NIV)

Reflection

There is no rest without release. We cannot receive peace while clinging to pressure.

Jesus invites us to come—not polished, not perfect, but weary. The only requirement is that we bring our burden and lay it down.

True rest begins with surrender. You don't have to carry what's crushing you. Let go. Unburden. Come.

Prayer

Jesus, I bring You my burden. I lay down what is too heavy to carry. Teach me to rest in You, not just beside You.

Prompt

What are you carrying that's too heavy for your soul? Write it down and surrender it to Jesus in prayer.

17

Cease Striving

Scripture

Psalm 46:10 - "Be still, and know that I am God." (NIV)

Reflection

Stillness isn't inactivity—it's intentional trust. It's the sacred pause that declares God is in control and we don't have to be.

Striving exhausts the soul. We strive to fix, to impress, to secure. But stillness allows us to recognise that He is already working.

To be still is to say, "I trust You, God, more than I trust my effort."

Prayer

Father, help me stop striving. Still my anxious heart. Let my stillness be an act of deep trust in Your goodness and power.

Prompt

Find a moment today to stop and be still. No fixing, no talking, just knowing He is God.

18

Yielding to the Shepherd

Scripture

John 10:11 - "I am the good shepherd. The good shepherd lays down his life for the sheep." (NIV)

Reflection

We like control. But sheep don't lead. They follow.

Jesus isn't just a rescuer—He's a shepherd. He leads gently, speaks lovingly, and protects fiercely. But we must yield.

Surrender isn't weakness. It's the strength to trust Someone wiser. The Shepherd knows the way. You were never meant to figure it all out alone.

Prayer

Good Shepherd, I yield to You. Lead me where You will. Help me to trust Your guidance more than my plans.

Prompt

Ask God where He's leading you in this season. What might yielding to Him look like today?

19

Not My Will

Scripture

Luke 22:42 - "Father, if you are willing, take this cup from me; yet not my will, but yours be done." (NIV)

Reflection

Surrender finds its fullest expression in Jesus. In Gethsemane, He faced agony, yet chose obedience.

Real surrender isn't about comfort—it's about yielding to a greater purpose. Sometimes the cup doesn't pass. Sometimes God's will leads through pain.

But even there, in the hardest surrender, we find divine strength. And resurrection always follows obedience.

Prayer

Lord, even when it's hard, help me to say, 'Not my will, but Yours.' Teach me to trust that Your plans are wiser than my desires.

Prompt

Is there an area where your will is resisting God's? Ask for grace to trust Him and surrender fully.

20

Trusting in the Quiet

Scripture

Isaiah 32:17 - "The fruit of that righteousness will be peace; its effect will be quietness and confidence forever." (NIV)

Reflection

God often works in the quiet—not with fireworks, but with fruit. Peace. Confidence. Assurance.

The world values noise and visibility, but heaven values trust and fruitfulness.

When you walk closely with God, you may not always feel loud confirmation. But the quiet within you will testify: you are where you're meant to be.

Prayer

God of peace, anchor me in Your quiet strength. Let my life bear the fruit of trust even when I can't see the full picture.

Prompt

Spend five minutes in silence. Ask God to show you the fruit He's producing in the quiet places of your life.

21

Open Hands, Open Heart

Scripture

Proverbs 3:5-6 - "Trust in the Lord with all your heart and lean not on your own understanding..." (NIV)

Reflection

Surrender begins with open hands. When we let go of understanding, control, and timing, we make room for God to move.

Open hands free the heart. Clenched fists can't receive. God wants not just your trust but your openness—your willingness to be led, shaped, and changed.

Let Him write the story. He knows the way, even when you do not.

Prayer

Lord, I open my hands today. I release control, fear, and the need to understand. Lead me. I trust You.

Prompt

Literally open your hands in prayer. What do you need to release today? Speak it aloud to God as an act of surrender.

22

Burned Out or Poured Out?

Scripture

2 Timothy 4:6 – "For I am already being poured out like a drink offering…" (NIV)

Reflection

There's a difference between being burned out and being poured out.

Burnout comes from striving in your own strength. Pouring out comes from abiding in God and offering yourself in His timing and power.

One depletes, the other overflows. Jesus was poured out, never burnt out. He moved in rest, acted in alignment, and withdrew to refill.

Let your surrender be a pouring, not a striving. Allow God determine the pace and the portion.

Prayer

Lord, I don't want to burn out trying to prove myself. Teach me to pour out my life from a place of rest and communion with You.

Prompt

Ask God: Am I living poured out or burnt out? What rhythms do I need to change to live from a place of rest?

23

The Humble Posture

Scripture

James 4:10 - "Humble yourselves before the Lord, and he will lift you up." (NIV)

Reflection

Surrender is rooted in humility. It says, 'God knows better. God leads better. God loves better.'

Humility is not thinking less of yourself—it's thinking rightly about yourself in light of God.

When we come low, God lifts us. When we stop pushing ourselves forward, He brings us exactly where we need to be.

Prayer

Jesus, teach me the way of humility. Let me bow low before You, trusting You to lift me in the right time and way.

Prompt

Reflect on an area where pride or control might be blocking surrender. Ask God for grace to choose humility.

24
Letting Go of Control

Scripture

Isaiah 55:8-9 - "For my thoughts are not your thoughts, neither are your ways my ways," declares the Lord." (NIV)

Reflection

Control feels safe—but it's an illusion. We were never meant to carry the weight of managing everything.

God's ways are higher, better, wiser. Letting go of control is an act of trust in His goodness and sovereignty.

When you stop trying to hold it all together, you make space for God to do what only He can do.

Prayer

God, I let go. I release the things I can't manage, fix, or understand. I trust Your higher ways and wiser thoughts.

Prompt

Write down three things you've been trying to control. Speak them aloud to God and place them in His hands.

25

Safe to Rest

Scripture

Psalm 4:8 - "In peace I will lie down and sleep, for you alone, Lord, make me dwell in safety." (NIV)

Reflection

Rest is hard when we don't feel safe. But God offers more than peace—He offers protection.

When we know we are held, we stop striving. When we trust that He watches over us, we can finally rest.

You are not alone in the night. You are not unguarded. The God who never sleeps is keeping watch over your soul.

Prayer

God of peace, help me to believe that I am safe in Your care. Let Your presence be my shield and Your love my covering.

Prompt

Tonight, before you sleep, speak this scripture aloud. Invite God to cover you in peace and let yourself rest deeply in Him.

26

When Obedience Feels Slow

Scripture

Hebrews 10:36 - "You need to persevere so that when you have done the will of God, you will receive what he has promised." (NIV)

Reflection

Sometimes obedience doesn't yield instant results. You say yes, and things still feel quiet, slow, or hidden.

But God sees. He honours every step. Obedience is never wasted—even when the fruit takes time to appear.

If you're walking in obedience, keep going. The promise is not just in the result—it's in the faithful journey with Him.

Prayer

Faithful God, remind me that slow obedience is still obedience. Help me persevere, even when I can't yet see the fruit.

Prompt

Think of something you've done in obedience that hasn't yet produced results. Write a prayer of trust to God about it.

27

The Art of Waiting on God

Scripture

Lamentations 3:25 - "The Lord is good to those whose hope is in him, to the one who seeks him." (NIV)

Reflection

Waiting is not passive—it's attentive. To wait on God is to seek Him with expectation, not frustration.

The soul that waits is the soul that watches. You become more aware, more present, more open to His whisper.

There is goodness in the waiting. Not just in what will come, but in how He reveals Himself while you wait.

Prayer

Lord, teach me to wait with purpose. Let my heart be attentive, expectant, and fully open to You in the in-between spaces.

Prompt

What does waiting on God look like for you right now? Journal about how He might be revealing His goodness in this season.

28

Grace in the Pause

Scripture

Exodus 33:14 - "The Lord replied, 'My Presence will go with you, and I will give you rest.'" (NIV)

Reflection

Pauses are not setbacks—they are sacred.

Sometimes God calls us to pause so we can realign with His presence, recalibrate our purpose, and receive His rest.

In the pause, we're reminded that our value doesn't come from constant motion but from constant communion.

Don't rush the pause. Grace lives there.

Prayer

Lord, thank You for the pauses. Help me not to resist them. Let me receive Your grace and rest in every moment You call me to stop.

Prompt

Where in your life is God inviting you to pause? Embrace it as a gift and reflect on what He might be saying in the stillness.

29

What Surrender Sounds Like

Scripture

1 Samuel 3:10 – "Speak, for your servant is listening." (NIV)

Reflection

Surrender often begins with listening. Before there's movement, there's a posture—a heart that says, 'I'm here. I'm listening. I'm willing.'

Samuel's surrender was simple but powerful. He didn't demand answers. He didn't offer plans. He simply made space for God to speak.

When we stop filling the silence with our own noise, we begin to hear the sound of surrender.

Prayer

Speak, Lord. I am listening. Quiet every other voice so I can hear and follow Yours with a surrendered heart.

Prompt

Spend time today listening in silence. Don't ask for anything. Just be present, and let your heart say, 'Your servant is listening.'

30

Resting as Worship

Scripture

Hebrews 4:10 - "For anyone who enters God's rest also rests from their works, just as God did from his." (NIV)

Reflection

Rest is not unspiritual. It is a form of worship—a declaration that God is enough and we are not our work.

When we rest in Him, we honour Him. We align our hearts with His rhythm and declare our dependence on His grace.

Don't just see rest as recovery. See it as reverence. Rest because God rested. Rest because He is worthy.

Prayer

God, I worship You by resting today. I lay down my striving and acknowledge that You are the source of all things.

Prompt

What would it look like to treat rest as an act of worship this week? Plan one intentional moment of rest with God.

PART THREE: PRESENCE
OVER PERFORMANCE

31

Mary Chose the Better Part

Scripture

Luke 10:42 - "But few things are needed—or indeed only one. Mary has chosen what is better, and it will not be taken away from her." (NIV)

Reflection

In a room full of distractions, Mary chose presence.

While Martha was busy doing for Jesus, Mary sat with Him. She wasn't lazy—she was longing. She didn't miss the moment.

Performance fades. Presence remains. Choosing the 'better part' means choosing relationship over reputation, communion over completion.

Jesus honours the one who sits before the one who serves in a rush.

Prayer

Jesus, help me choose what is better. Teach me to sit at Your feet before I run with tasks. Let me delight in being with You more than doing for You.

Prompt

Think of one way you can prioritise presence with Jesus this week. What might you need to pause or let go of to do so?

32

Presence is the Prize

Scripture

Psalm 16:11 - "You make known to me the path of life; you will fill me with joy in your presence…" (NIV)

Reflection

We often chase outcomes, answers, and direction. But what if the path of life isn't found in clarity, but in closeness?

God's presence is not a means to an end—it is the end. It's the prize. The reward. The joy.

Don't rush past His presence looking for something else. Everything you need is found there.

Prayer

Lord, make me hungry for Your presence. Let me see it as the greatest treasure. Fill me with joy that comes only from nearness to You.

Prompt

Pause and reflect: Have you been seeking God's hand more than His face? What might change if His presence became your greatest desire?

33

The Table Before Me

Scripture

Psalm 23:5 - "You prepare a table before me in the presence of my enemies…" (NIV)

Reflection

Even in the middle of battle, God invites you to sit and eat.

He doesn't remove every enemy—He invites you into peace anyway. The table represents fellowship, provision, and stillness.

Performance says, 'Fight harder.' Presence says, 'Come and dine.' Let the Shepherd prepare the table. Your place is already set.

Prayer

Shepherd of my soul, help me sit at Your table even when life is loud. Let me rest in Your presence, knowing I am held and fed by You.

Prompt

Imagine the table God has set for you today. What does it look like to pause and receive from Him instead of striving?

34

Unseen, Yet Held

Scripture

Colossians 3:3 - "For you died, and your life is now hidden with Christ in God." (NIV)

Reflection

The unhurried life often feels hidden—unseen by the world, unnoticed by others. But hidden does not mean forgotten.

God sees you. He holds your life in His hands, even when no one else notices your obedience, your tears, or your quiet yes.

You are hidden with Christ. And that's the safest, most sacred place to be.

Prayer

Father, thank You for seeing me when no one else does. Help me to find joy in being hidden with You rather than seeking recognition.

Prompt

Reflect on an area of your life where you feel unseen. Ask God to help you see His presence and purpose there.

35

No Need to Impress

Scripture

Galatians 1:10 - "Am I now trying to win the approval of human beings, or of God?" (NIV)

Reflection

The pressure to impress is exhausting. But in the presence of God, there's no need to perform.

He already knows you—completely—and loves you deeply. You don't have to earn what He's already given freely.

True rest begins when you stop performing and start abiding. Allow God's approval be enough.

Prayer

God, deliver me from the need to impress. Help me find peace in Your love and rest in the truth that I am already accepted.

Prompt

Where in your life are you striving to prove something? Release that area to God and ask Him to redefine your worth.

36

Dwelling with God

Scripture

Psalm 91:1 – "Whoever dwells in the shelter of the Most High will rest in the shadow of the Almighty." (NIV)

Reflection

There's a difference between visiting God and dwelling with Him.

Dwelling speaks of staying, settling, being rooted in relationship. It's not a once-a-week encounter—it's a way of life.

When you dwell with God, you carry His presence into every moment. You live in the shadow of His peace, even in the heat of life.

Prayer

Lord, teach me to dwell with You—to live in constant awareness of Your nearness. Let my life be anchored in Your shelter.

Prompt

How can you shift from visiting God to dwelling with Him? Write down one way you'll cultivate daily presence this week.

37

Staying When It's Boring

Scripture

Isaiah 40:31 - "But those who wait on the Lord will renew their strength..." (NIV)

Reflection

Not every moment in God's presence feels dramatic. Sometimes it feels quiet. Ordinary. Even boring.

But the unhurried soul learns to stay. To wait. To trust that even in silence, God is at work.

Spiritual depth is formed in the moments we choose to stay—not because we feel something, but because we love Someone.

Prayer

God, help me to stay with You even when I don't feel anything. Teach me that Your presence is enough, even in the quiet and the mundane.

Prompt

Have you been tempted to leave your quiet time early? Try staying a little longer today, even in silence.

38

Holy Ground is Ordinary

Scripture

Exodus 3:5 - "Take off your sandals, for the place where you are standing is holy ground." (NIV)

Reflection

Moses wasn't in a temple. He was in the wilderness when God called the ground holy.

God meets us in ordinary places—kitchens, cars, quiet corners. When He shows up, even the mundane becomes sacred.

You don't need a perfect setting to encounter Him. You just need eyes to see and a heart that's ready.

Prayer

Lord, open my eyes to see You in the everyday. Let me recognise Your presence in the ordinary places of my life.

Prompt

Look around your surroundings right now. Ask God to show you how this space might become holy ground today.

39

Praying Without Performing

Scripture

Matthew 6:6 - "But when you pray, go into your room, close the door and pray to your Father, who is unseen…" (NIV)

Reflection

Prayer isn't a performance. It's a conversation with the One who knows you already.

God isn't impressed by fancy words or long speeches. He's drawn to honesty, vulnerability, and presence.

You don't need to sound holy to be heard. You just need to be real. Unhurried prayer is unpolished prayer—it's personal, simple, true.

Prayer

Father, strip away the need to perform in prayer. Teach me to speak with You simply, openly, and with my whole heart.

Prompt

Try praying today without a script. Just speak to God like a child would speak to their loving parent.

40

The Smile of God

Scripture

Numbers 6:25 - "The Lord make his face shine on you and be gracious to you." (NIV)

Reflection

God's presence isn't just power—it's delight.

To be in God's presence is to be under His smile. His face shines with grace, with joy, with love toward His children.

When we slow down to seek Him, we discover He is not distant or displeased—He is beaming with affection.

You are not just tolerated. You are treasured.

Prayer

Lord, help me to live under Your smile. Let Your delight quiet my striving and Your joy renew my spirit.

Prompt

Take a few minutes to picture God smiling over you. Let that image shape the way you pray and live today.

41

More Than Productivity

Scripture

John 15:5 - "Apart from me you can do nothing." (NIV)

Reflection

In a world that praises productivity, Jesus reminds us that fruit comes from connection—not effort alone.

You were not created to be a machine. You were created to abide. And from that place of abiding, true fruit will grow.

Being with Jesus matters more than doing for Him. Slow down. Stay close. He's the vine—you're the branch.

Prayer

Jesus, teach me to abide rather than perform. Let my life flow from connection, not pressure. You are enough.

Prompt

Review your to-do list today. What could be set aside to make more room for simply being with God?

42

He Sees Me

Scripture

Genesis 16:13 - "She gave this name to the Lord who spoke to her: 'You are the God who sees me...'" (NIV)

Reflection

Hagar wasn't in a sanctuary—she was in the wilderness. Yet even there, God saw her.

He sees you too. Not just the part of you that shows up polished and prayerful, but the whole you.

In your wandering, weeping, or wondering, He sees. And His seeing isn't passive—it's full of compassion and care.

Prayer

God who sees, thank You for noticing me. For caring. For drawing near. Help me to rest in the assurance that I am never out of Your sight.

Prompt

Spend a few minutes journaling: 'God sees me in...' and complete the sentence with honesty and gratitude.

43

Attention is Worship

Scripture

Proverbs 4:25 – "Let your eyes look straight ahead; fix your gaze directly before you." (NIV)

Reflection

In a distracted world, focused attention is a rare offering.

God longs not just for your time but for your attention—undivided, present, and sincere.

When you fix your gaze on Him, it becomes worship. Even without words, your presence becomes a prayer.

Attention isn't a small thing. It's sacred.

Prayer

God, I bring You my full attention. Teach me to turn from distractions and focus on Your presence with honour and joy.

Prompt

What's been stealing your attention lately? Choose one way to minimise distraction today and give God your full gaze.

44

Practicing Presence

Scripture

1 Thessalonians 5:17 - "Pray continually." (NIV)

Reflection

Continual prayer isn't about speaking non-stop—it's about living aware.

God is always with you. Practicing His presence means acknowledging Him in the small things, not just the spiritual ones.

The more you practice His presence, the more it becomes natural. Not forced. Not religious. Just real.

Prayer

Lord, help me live in constant awareness of You. Let my everyday moments become sacred as I walk with You.

Prompt

Pause during your day and whisper, 'You are here.' Let that be a doorway into deeper communion.

45

When All You Can Do is Sit

Scripture

Romans 8:26 - "The Spirit helps us in our weakness. We do not know what we ought to pray for, but the Spirit himself intercedes for us…" (NIV)

Reflection

There are days when prayer feels impossible. When words won't come, and all you can do is sit.

That's okay. God understands. The Spirit intercedes in sighs and silence.

Sometimes, the holiest thing you can do is show up. Sit. Breathe. Be.

God is present in that space, every time.

Prayer

Holy Spirit, thank You for praying when I have no words. Meet me in my silence and make it sacred.

Prompt

Set aside five minutes today to simply sit with God. No pressure. Just presence.

46

He Delights to Be With You

Scripture

Zephaniah 3:17 - "The Lord your God is with you… he will take great delight in you…" (NIV)

Reflection

God doesn't just tolerate your presence–He delights in it.

When you come to Him, even with weariness or weakness, He rejoices. His love is not reluctant but rejoicing.

Let this truth quiet your striving. You are not a burden to God. You are His beloved, and He delights to be near you.

Prayer

God, thank You for delighting in me. Help me to rest in Your joy and respond to Your love with openness and trust.

Prompt

Spend a moment reflecting on the word 'delight.' What does it mean to you that God delights in you, not just loves you?

47

The Ministry of Stillness

Scripture

Exodus 14:14 - "The Lord will fight for you; you need only to be still." (NIV)

Reflection

Sometimes the greatest act of faith is to be still.

We want to act, fix, respond—but God often invites us to stillness. Not because there's nothing to do, but because He is already working.

Stillness can be ministry. It says, 'God is enough. I trust Him here.' Let your stillness become a testimony.

Prayer

Fighting God, help me to be still when You say still. Teach me to trust Your strength over my striving.

Prompt

In what area of life is God calling you to stillness rather than action? Write a prayer of trust for that space.

48

Rest is Relational

Scripture

Matthew 11:29 - "Take my yoke upon you and learn from me... and you will find rest for your souls." (NIV)

Reflection

Rest isn't found in escape—it's found in relationship.

Jesus invites us into rest by walking with Him, not running from life. His yoke is not weightless, but it is shared.

When you walk in step with Christ, you learn what it means to move in grace and live in peace.

Real rest is found in staying close to the One who carries the weight with you.

Prayer

Jesus, help me to walk with You. Let me find rest not just in stopping, but in surrendering to Your rhythm.

Prompt

What does walking in step with Jesus look like in your current season? Reflect on how His rhythm might differ from yours.

49

Tending to the Inner Life

Scripture

Proverbs 4:23 - "Above all else, guard your heart, for everything you do flows from it." (NIV)

Reflection

The unhurried life requires inner attentiveness.

We often focus on outward tasks and forget the soul that drives them. But your inner life is the wellspring of your actions.

To live slowly with God means to check in with your heart—regularly, honestly, tenderly. Guard it not by fear, but by faith and intentional care.

Prayer

Lord, help me tend to my inner life. Teach me to guard my heart with wisdom and grace, and let Your peace reign within me.

Prompt

Take time to reflect on your inner world today. How is your heart really doing? Bring it honestly before God.

50

God is in the Room

Scripture

Genesis 28:16 - "Surely the Lord is in this place, and I was not aware of it." (NIV)

Reflection

Jacob woke up to a divine reality—God had been present, and he didn't even know it.

How many rooms, moments, or meetings have we rushed through unaware?

God is not distant. He is present—in every space, every breath, every detail. The invitation is not to bring Him in, but to notice He's already here.

Prayer

Lord, awaken me to Your presence. Let me not rush past holy moments. Help me recognise that You are in the room with me, always.

Prompt

Before your next task, pause. Whisper, 'God is here.' May that truth shape how you engage the moment.

PART FOUR: ABIDE

51

Abide in Me

Scripture

John 15:4 - "Remain in me, as I also remain in you. No branch can bear fruit by itself..." (NIV)

Reflection

To abide is to stay—rooted, connected, and dependent.

Jesus doesn't invite us to occasionally visit Him. He calls us to remain, to make our home in Him. In this union, we find nourishment, strength, and fruitfulness.

The unhurried life begins here—in abiding, not striving. You don't grow by force, but by staying connected to the Vine.

Prayer

Jesus, I choose to remain in You. Let my heart stay rooted in Your love, my life in step with Your presence.

Prompt

What helps you stay connected to Jesus throughout the day? Reflect on one way you can abide more fully this week.

52

Union Not Transaction

Scripture

1 Corinthians 6:17 - "But whoever is united with the Lord is one with him in spirit." (NIV)

Reflection

God doesn't want a transaction—He desires union.

We're not called to spiritual exchanges but spiritual intimacy. Union means shared life, shared heart, shared rhythm.

You are not a client of God's grace—you're a participant in His love. And He longs to dwell with you, not just work for you.

Prayer

Lord, draw me deeper into union with You. Let me walk in the reality of shared life, not just requests.

Prompt

Today, focus on being with God more than asking from Him. How does this shift your heart posture?

53

Vines and Branches

Scripture

John 15:5 - "I am the vine; you are the branches. If you remain in me and I in you, you will bear much fruit..." (NIV)

Reflection

The branch doesn't produce fruit by effort—it bears fruit by connection.

As long as it stays attached to the vine, growth happens naturally. Our job is not to force fruit but to remain in Christ.

Unhurried living means trusting that abiding is enough. God brings the growth. We bring the willingness to stay connected.

Prayer

Jesus, keep me connected to You. Let every part of my life draw nourishment from our union. Bear fruit through me in Your time and way.

Prompt

How are you currently staying attached to the Vine? Are there areas where you've been trying to grow without connection?

54

Closeness Without Clamour

Scripture

Psalm 131:2 - "But I have calmed and quieted myself, I am like a weaned child with its mother..." (NIV)

Reflection

There is a kind of closeness with God that doesn't demand or strive—it simply rests.

Like a child who no longer cries for milk but simply enjoys the comfort of being near, we too can find peace in presence without performance.

Abiding sometimes looks like stillness. Quiet. Calm. The intimacy of being near without needing anything more than Him.

Prayer

God, calm my heart. Teach me to enjoy being with You without needing to do, ask, or prove. Let me rest in Your nearness.

Prompt

Sit with God in silence today for a few minutes. No words— just closeness. What does that kind of quiet communion feel like?

55

A Life Rooted in Love

Scripture

Ephesians 3:17 - "And I pray that you, being rooted and established in love..." (NIV)

Reflection

To abide is to root your life in love—not in fear, effort, or approval.

When your roots go deep into God's love, you are nourished, sustained, and unshaken by the storms around you.

Let love—not anxiety—be the soil you grow in. Abiding in love brings peace, purpose, and fruit that lasts.

Prayer

Lord, root me in Your love. Let everything in my life be grounded in the truth that I am fully known and fully loved by You.

Prompt

Ask God to show you where your life is rooted. Are you growing from love, or from fear and striving?

56

No Branch Bears Fruit Alone

Scripture

John 15:4 - "No branch can bear fruit by itself; it must remain in the vine." (NIV)

Reflection

Independence sounds strong, but in the Kingdom, fruitfulness is born from dependence.

You were never meant to produce fruit alone. Your strength, peace, wisdom, and impact flow from union with Christ.

Abiding is not weakness—it is wisdom. Stay connected. You're not designed to do this alone.

Prayer

Jesus, I release my need to do it all on my own. I stay connected to You today. Let all I do flow from Your life within me.

Prompt

Is there an area where you've been operating independently of God? Invite Him back into that space today.

57

Remaining When It's Hard

Scripture

John 6:68 - "Lord, to whom shall we go? You have the words of eternal life." (NIV)

Reflection

Sometimes abiding isn't peaceful—it's painful.

It means staying when prayers go unanswered. Trusting when feelings fade. Holding on when walking away feels easier.

But like Peter, we discover there's nowhere else to go. Abiding is choosing Jesus over comfort, consistency over clarity.

Even when it's hard, His presence is still our home.

Prayer

Lord, help me remain when it's hard. Give me the strength to abide in You when everything in me wants to run.

Prompt

Where in your life is it hard to remain with God? Write an honest prayer of surrender and trust.

58

A Rhythm of Remaining

Scripture

Galatians 5:25 - "Since we live by the Spirit, let us keep in step with the Spirit." (NIV)

Reflection

Abiding is not just a moment—it's a rhythm.

It's a way of walking with God daily, learning His pace and posture.

Remaining means choosing communion over chaos, slowing your steps to stay in sync with His Spirit.

Keep in step. Let the Spirit lead, not just visit.

Prayer

Spirit of God, set the rhythm of my life. Help me walk with You, not ahead of You. Let Your pace become my peace.

Prompt

What would it look like to let the Holy Spirit set your rhythm today? Write a few words or phrases that describe His pace.

59

Sit Before You Serve

Scripture

Mark 3:14 – "He appointed twelve that they might be with him and that he might send them out…" (NIV)

Reflection

Before the disciples were sent out, they were called to be with Jesus.

Presence precedes purpose. Ministry flows from intimacy. When you sit with Him first, your service becomes overflow, not obligation.

Don't skip the sitting. Let being with Him shape what you do for Him.

Prayer

Jesus, let me be with You before I serve You. Teach me to sit in Your presence and let all I do flow from our connection.

Prompt

Reflect on this: Are you sitting before you're serving? What might need to shift in your schedule to prioritise presence?

60

Fruit Comes Slow

Scripture

James 5:7 - "See how the farmer waits for the land to yield its valuable crop, patiently waiting for the autumn and spring rains." (NIV)

Reflection

Fruit doesn't come overnight. It takes time—seasons of watering, waiting, and trusting.

The world rewards fast results, but God forms lasting fruit. Don't despise the slowness. Every quiet moment of abiding is cultivating something eternal.

Allow your soul grow like a tree—deep roots, slow growth, lasting fruit.

Prayer

God, help me to be patient in the process. Let me trust Your timing and stay rooted in You, even when the growth feels slow.

Prompt

What fruit are you hoping to see in this season? Write a prayer of trust over that area.

61

The Long Obedience

Scripture

Romans 2:7 - "To those who by persistence in doing good seek glory, honor and immortality, he will give eternal life." (NIV)

Reflection

Abiding is not flashy—it's faithful. It's the long obedience in the same direction.

There may be no applause, no spotlight, no fast reward. But there is glory in the unseen endurance of a soul that keeps saying yes.

God sees your steady walk. Keep going. Faithfulness is never wasted.

Prayer

Lord, make me faithful. Give me grace to walk steadily with You, even when it's quiet and unseen. I want to endure with joy.

Prompt

Think of one area where you've been walking faithfully. Thank God for the strength to persist and ask for renewed endurance.

62

Quiet Confidence

Scripture

Isaiah 30:15 - "In quietness and trust is your strength…" (NIV)

Reflection

Abiding produces confidence—not loud or arrogant, but quiet and unshakable.

When your soul is anchored in God, you don't need to prove, push, or panic. You rest. You trust.

True strength isn't always seen—it's felt in the calm courage of a heart held by God.

Prayer

God, grow in me a quiet confidence. Let my strength come from trust, not control. Help me walk in calm assurance that You are with me.

Prompt

Where do you need quiet confidence today? Write a declaration of trust based on God's promises.

63

Water the Roots

Scripture

Jeremiah 17:8 - "They will be like a tree planted by the water… its roots by the stream…" (NIV)

Reflection

The health of a tree depends on the strength of its roots.

When you take time to water your inner life—through prayer, worship, stillness—you prepare for fruitfulness that lasts through every season.

Don't just focus on what's seen. Tend to what's hidden. That's where the life flows from.

Prayer

Lord, help me to care for the roots of my soul. Keep me planted near Your living water, and grow something deep and lasting in me.

Prompt

How are you watering your spiritual roots right now? What practices help nourish your soul beneath the surface?

64

Don't Rush the Rain

Scripture

Hosea 6:3 - "As surely as the sun rises, he will appear; he will come to us like the winter rains…" (NIV)

Reflection

Rain doesn't come on demand. It comes in season.

You can't force spiritual growth or manufacture revival. But you can stay expectant. Stay open. Stay present.

God will come—like the rain—at just the right time. Let the waiting prepare your soil, not harden your heart.

Prayer

Faithful God, I trust Your timing. Teach me not to rush the rain, but to wait in hope and prepare my heart to receive.

Prompt

What does it look like for you to prepare for the rain in your life? Reflect on what God may be nurturing in the waiting.

65

Dwelling in the Word

Scripture

Colossians 3:16 - "Let the word of Christ dwell in you richly..." (NIV)

Reflection

The Word isn't meant to be rushed through—it's meant to dwell.

When **Scripture** lives inside you, it nourishes, shapes, and transforms. One verse can feed your soul more than a hundred rushed chapters.

Read slowly. Linger long. Allow the Word take up residence and bear fruit in every corner of your heart.

Prayer

Lord, let Your Word dwell in me. Not just visit, but live deep in my soul. Teach me to listen slowly and receive fully.

Prompt

Choose one verse today and read it slowly several times. Let it dwell in you, and write what you hear God saying through it.

66

The Fruit of Abiding

Scripture

Galatians 5:22-23 - "But the fruit of the Spirit is love, joy, peace, forbearance, kindness, goodness, faithfulness, gentleness and self-control…" (NIV)

Reflection

The fruit of the Spirit doesn't grow from striving—it grows from abiding.

When you remain in Christ, these virtues begin to flourish—not as forced behaviours but as natural evidence of life in the Vine.

Check the fruit not to judge, but to discern: Am I staying close to Jesus? Fruitfulness is a by-product of friendship with Him.

Prayer

Holy Spirit, produce Your fruit in me. Let love and joy and peace grow as I abide in Christ today.

Prompt

Which fruit of the Spirit do you long to see more of in your life? Ask God to cultivate it through your abiding.

67

When You Feel Disconnected

Scripture

Psalm 63:1 - "You, God, are my God, earnestly I seek you...
in a dry and parched land where there is no water." (NIV)

Reflection

Even those who love God deeply can go through seasons
of dryness.

Disconnection isn't failure—it's a moment for redirection.
When you feel distant, seek Him. Return. Reconnect.

God has not moved away. He is near, ready to restore
the flow. Don't run from the dryness—let it deepen your
desire.

Prayer

Lord, when I feel dry or distant, draw me back. Reconnect
my heart to Yours and help me seek You earnestly again.

Prompt

Be honest with God about where you feel disconnected.
Invite Him to restore closeness, even if you don't feel it
yet.

68
Restoring the Flow

Scripture

Revelation 2:4-5 - "Yet I hold this against you: You have forsaken the love you had at first..." (NIV)

Reflection

Sometimes we lose connection not from rebellion, but from routine.

God calls us back—not to shame us, but to restore us. Return to your first love. Return to delight, to desire, to deep dependence.

Abiding isn't about trying harder—it's about coming closer. Let the flow return through repentance and renewed affection.

Prayer

Jesus, I return to You. Restore the love I had at first. Let my heart beat again with longing for You above all else.

Prompt

What would it look like for you to return to your first love today? Make one small move back toward intimacy.

69

The Joy of Being With Him

Scripture

Psalm 16:11 - "In your presence there is fullness of joy…" (NIV)

Reflection

Abiding isn't a duty—it's a delight.

God's presence is not a place of pressure, but of pleasure. Joy flows when we stop striving and simply enjoy Him.

Return to the joy of just being with God. Let it renew your strength and restore your wonder.

Prayer

God, restore to me the joy of being with You. Let Your presence lift my soul and fill me with deep, lasting joy.

Prompt

What brings you joy in God's presence? Reflect on or engage in one joyful practice with Him today.

70

Staying When It's Silent

Scripture

Lamentations 3:26 – "It is good to wait quietly for the salvation of the Lord." (NIV)

Reflection

Silence doesn't mean absence.

Sometimes God is quiet, not because He has left, but because He's deepening the roots of trust.

Abiding means staying, even when we don't hear. Even when we don't feel. The silence can still be sacred if we stay close.

Prayer

Lord, help me stay in the silence. Teach me to wait quietly, trusting You even when my heart longs for a word.

Prompt

How do you usually respond when God feels silent? Ask Him for grace to remain and trust in the quiet.

71

From Abiding to Overflow

Scripture

John 7:38 - "Whoever believes in me… rivers of living water will flow from within them." (NIV)

Reflection

Abiding doesn't end with stillness—it leads to overflow.

As you stay close to Jesus, His Spirit flows through you. Not a trickle, but rivers. You become a vessel of peace, joy, and life for others.

Let the overflow bless others, but never at the cost of connection. Keep coming back to the Source.

Prayer

Jesus, fill me again. Let Your Spirit flow through me—not by effort but by abiding. Make my life a river of living water.

Prompt

Who around you needs the overflow of your abiding? Ask God how you can pour out without drying up.

72

Rooted in Love, Again

Scripture

Ephesians 3:18-19 - "That you… may have power… to grasp how wide and long and high and deep is the love of Christ…" (NIV)

Reflection

We never outgrow the need to return to love.

When life gets rushed or dry, the remedy isn't more effort—it's deeper roots. Allow your soul be soaked again in the vastness of Christ's love.

The more rooted you are, the more you can withstand and flourish. Return to love. Abide in it.

Prayer

Jesus, root me again in Your love. Let me feel its depth, rest in its strength, and live out of its abundance.

Prompt

Write down what you know to be true about God's love for you. Let those truths steady and fill you today.

73

Allow the Word Breathe

Scripture

2 Timothy 3:16 - "All **Scripture** is God-breathed and is useful…" (NIV)

Reflection

The Word isn't just ink on a page—it's breath. Life. Spirit.

When you sit with it unhurried, it exhales peace, conviction, clarity. You don't need to rush through chapters—just let it breathe in you.

A single verse, received slowly, can shape your soul more than a hurried study ever could.

Prayer

Holy Spirit, breathe through the Word as I read. Let it speak to the depths of me, and let me receive it with wonder.

Prompt

Choose one verse to sit with today. Read it slowly, aloud if you can, and ask: What are You breathing into me through this?

74

In Step With the Spirit

Scripture

Romans 8:14 - "For those who are led by the Spirit of God are the children of God." (NIV)

Reflection

Abiding is walking in step with the Spirit—not dragging ahead, not lagging behind.

It's learning His rhythm, His whisper, His timing. Life in the Spirit isn't about pressure—it's about partnership.

Let the Spirit lead. He knows where you're going, and He walks with grace.

Prayer

Spirit of God, lead me. Help me walk in step with You—no rushing, no resisting, just trusting.

Prompt

What might the Spirit be prompting you toward or away from today? Ask for ears to hear and feet to follow.

75

The Gift of Unfinished

Scripture

Philippians 1:6 - "He who began a good work in you will carry it on to completion…" (NIV)

Reflection

You are a work in progress—and that's a gift.

God never rushes transformation. He begins a good work, and He promises to finish it in His time.

You don't have to be perfect today. You're being formed. Loved in the process. Held in grace. May that truth quiet your striving.

Prayer

Lord, thank You for being patient with me. Help me to trust the process and rest in the promise that You will complete what You've started.

Prompt

Where are you putting pressure on yourself to be 'done'? Release it and thank God that you're still becoming.

76

The Strength of Stillness

Scripture

Isaiah 30:15 - "In repentance and rest is your salvation, in quietness and trust is your strength…" (NIV)

Reflection

Stillness isn't weakness—it's strength.

Not everyone will understand your pace. But those who walk with God learn to draw strength from stillness, not speed.

The unhurried soul is not lazy—it is deeply rooted. Grounded. Trusting. Strong in ways the world can't measure.

Prayer

Father, strengthen me in stillness. Teach me to draw from Your quiet power rather than my noisy efforts.

Prompt

What does stillness look like for you today? How can you lean into it as a source of strength rather than resistance?

77

A Soul That's Not in a Hurry

Scripture

Psalm 62:5 - "Yes, my soul, find rest in God; my hope comes from him." (NIV)

Reflection

The unhurried soul is rare—but it is beautiful.

It's not indifferent or lazy. It's anchored. Peaceful. Confident in God's timing.

You don't have to match the world's pace. Allow your soul find rest. And from that place, live and lead with calm, clarity, and courage.

Prayer

God, make my soul unhurried. Let me find my rest and hope in You alone. Quiet every rushing voice within me.

Prompt

Speak to your soul today like the psalmist: 'Find rest in God.' What would change if you lived from that place today?

78

Breathe Again

Scripture

Ezekiel 37:5 - "This is what the Sovereign Lord says to these bones: I will make breath enter you, and you will come to life." (NIV)

Reflection

Sometimes your soul feels dry. Like bones in a valley, lifeless and weary.

But God speaks breath. His Spirit brings life where fatigue has settled.

Abiding means letting Him breathe into the places you thought were too far gone. His breath revives. Receive it. Breathe again.

Prayer

Holy Spirit, breathe into my soul. Awaken what has grown dry and weary. Let me come alive in Your presence again.

Prompt

Take five deep, slow breaths. With each inhale, invite God's Spirit to fill you. With each exhale, release your weariness.

79

Let the Silence Speak

Scripture

Habakkuk 2:20 - "But the Lord is in his holy temple; let all the earth be silent before him." (NIV)

Reflection

Silence isn't empty—it's full of presence.

In silence, God speaks in ways our ears can't always hear but our souls recognise.

Let the silence stretch. Let it slow you. Let it speak. The unhurried heart knows that sometimes, silence is the holiest sound.

Prayer

God of silence, meet me in the quiet. Let me not run from stillness but sit with You there until I sense Your nearness.

Prompt

Set a timer for three minutes. Sit in silence before God. No requests. No music. Just presence. What did you notice?

80

Staying with the Shepherd

Scripture

John 10:27 - "My sheep listen to my voice; I know them, and they follow me." (NIV)

Reflection

Abiding means staying close enough to hear the Shepherd's voice.

It's not always loud. Sometimes it's a whisper. But His voice brings comfort, direction, and peace.

Let His nearness lead you. You don't need a map when you're walking with the One who knows the way.

Prayer

Jesus, my Shepherd, help me stay close enough to hear You. Let Your voice guide every step, and give me courage to follow.

Prompt

Where might the Shepherd be leading you right now? Listen closely. Write what you sense, even if it's just one word.

81

The Slow Grace of Healing

Scripture

Jeremiah 30:17 - "But I will restore you to health and heal your wounds,' declares the Lord..." (NIV)

Reflection

Healing rarely happens all at once. It's a slow grace.

God tends to our wounds like a careful gardener—gently, thoroughly, over time. Don't rush the process.

Abide in His love. Let His presence mend what's broken. Trust that restoration is happening, even if you can't yet see it.

Prayer

Lord, I welcome Your slow healing. Touch every wounded place with Your mercy and make me whole in Your time and way.

Prompt

What needs healing in your life right now? Write a simple prayer inviting God into that space with patience and hope.

82

Resting in the Mystery

Scripture

Ecclesiastes 11:5 – "As you do not know the path of the wind… so you cannot understand the work of God…" (NIV)

Reflection

You don't have to understand everything to rest in God.

Abiding often means surrendering the need to know. Trusting God's mystery more than your own clarity.

There's peace in letting go of the why and resting in the Who. He is good. That's enough.

Prayer

God, I release my need to understand. I rest in the mystery and trust in Your goodness. You are enough for me.

Prompt

What unanswered questions are weighing on you? Hand them over to God today and rest in His mystery.

83

Enough for Today

Scripture

Matthew 6:34 - "Therefore do not worry about tomorrow, for tomorrow will worry about itself…" (NIV)

Reflection

God gives grace one day at a time.

Abiding is not about stockpiling strength for the future. It's about trusting there will be enough for today—and tomorrow, He'll meet you again.

Stay in the moment. Breathe the grace that's here. Today is enough, and so is He.

Prayer

Father, thank You for daily grace. Help me to live in this moment with You and not be overwhelmed by what's ahead.

Prompt

What is your soul carrying that belongs to tomorrow? Speak a prayer of release and choose to walk with God just for today.

84

Weaned from Worry

Scripture

Matthew 6:27 - "Can any one of you by worrying add a single hour to your life?" (NIV)

Reflection

Worry feeds on hurry. The more anxious we are, the faster we move.

But Jesus calls us to a different rhythm—one of trust, not tension.

To be weaned from worry is to be nourished by His peace. The unhurried soul doesn't carry what it was never meant to hold.

Prayer

Lord, wean me from worry. Replace every anxious thought with the peace of knowing You are in control.

Prompt

What are you worrying about today? Speak it aloud and hand it over to the Lord who already sees and knows.

85

Holding Things Lightly

Scripture

Philippians 4:5 - "Let your gentleness be evident to all. The Lord is near." (NIV)

Reflection

The unhurried soul holds things lightly–plans, outcomes, expectations.

There's a gentleness that comes when you trust the nearness of God. You don't have to grip everything tightly.

Allow your hands relax. Allow your heart breathe. The Lord is near, and that is enough.

Prayer

God, help me hold all things lightly today. Let Your nearness be the anchor that steadies me in peace and gentleness.

Prompt

Take a few moments to open your hands. What are you gripping that you need to release? Practice holding it lightly in trust.

86

In the Stillness, He Builds

Scripture

Psalm 127:1 - "Unless the Lord builds the house, the builders labour in vain." (NIV)

Reflection

Sometimes doing less is actually trusting more.

When you step back, God steps in. Stillness isn't idleness—it's space for Him to build what you cannot.

The unhurried heart learns that God's hands are more capable than our hustle.

Prayer

Master Builder, I give You space to work. Teach me to pause and let You construct what truly lasts.

Prompt

Where might God be inviting you to pause and let Him build? Write a prayer of release over that area.

87

Faith Moves Slowly

Scripture

Hebrews 11:8 - "By faith Abraham… went out, not knowing where he was going." (NIV)

Reflection

Faith doesn't always rush forward—it often moves slowly, step by step.

Abraham obeyed without knowing the full map. He trusted the One leading him more than the path itself.

The unhurried life walks in faith, not certainty. Let go of needing to know everything. God's pace is still faithful.

Prayer

God of Abraham, help me trust You even when I don't have all the answers. Let my faith move slowly and steadily with You.

Prompt

What step of faith are you taking without clarity? Name it before God and ask for grace to walk slowly and trust deeply.

88

Come Back to Rest

Scripture

Psalm 116:7 - "Return to your rest, my soul, for the Lord has been good to you." (NIV)

Reflection

Sometimes our soul forgets to rest.

We drift into striving or anxiety. But the invitation remains: Come back. Return to rest. God has not changed.

His goodness is still your anchor. His faithfulness still your foundation. You can return—even now.

Prayer

Lord, I bring my soul back to You. Remind me of Your goodness and let me find rest again in Your presence.

Prompt

Where has your soul wandered away from rest? Speak Psalm 116:7 over yourself today as a declaration and invitation.

89

When God Waits With You

Scripture

Isaiah 64:4 - "No eye has seen... a God who acts on behalf of those who wait for him." (NIV)

Reflection

Waiting feels lonely—but you are not alone.

God doesn't just wait for you to act; He waits with you. He is present in the delay, active in the unseen.

His companionship in the waiting is part of the miracle. You may be still, but He is not inactive.

Prayer

God, thank You for waiting with me. Help me to rest in Your presence as I trust in Your timing and activity.

Prompt

Reflect: How does it change your experience of waiting to know God is waiting with you, not just for you?

90

Grace for Small Beginnings

Scripture

Zechariah 4:10 - "Do not despise these small beginnings, for the Lord rejoices to see the work begin…" (NIV)

Reflection

We often overlook the small because we long for the significant.

But God rejoices in small beginnings. He delights in every quiet start, unseen step, and faithful seed.

Abiding means trusting that God is present in the process—not just the product.

Prayer

Lord, thank You for small beginnings. Help me not to rush or despise what You are growing slowly in me.

Prompt

What small beginning are you in right now? Invite God to bless it, breathe on it, and remind you He rejoices over it.

91

Hidden but Growing

Scripture

Mark 4:27 - "Night and day… the seed sprouts and grows, though he does not know how." (NIV)

Reflection

Growth doesn't always look like progress.

Much of God's work in us happens beneath the surface, hidden but holy. Trust that the seeds are sprouting—even when you don't see movement.

Abiding gives space for invisible growth. Allow God work in the quiet soil of your soul.

Prayer

God, grow what I cannot see. Help me trust the hidden work You are doing in and through me.

Prompt

Think of an area where growth feels slow or invisible. Write a prayer of trust for what's taking root beneath the surface.

92

Follow the Cloud

Scripture

Exodus 40:36 - "In all the travels of the Israelites, whenever the cloud lifted... they would set out." (NIV)

Reflection

God's people moved with the cloud, not their own plans.

The unhurried life watches for God's leading–not rushing ahead or lagging behind. He knows when to move and when to stay.

Allow God set the pace. Follow the cloud, not the crowd.

Prayer

Lord, help me follow Your lead. Let me move when You move and wait when You wait. I trust Your timing more than my plans.

Prompt

What 'cloud' are you watching in this season? Spend a moment asking God where He is leading you now.

93

Letting Go of the Outcome

Scripture

Proverbs 16:9 - "In their hearts humans plan their course, but the Lord establishes their steps." (NIV)

Reflection

You can obey and still not control the outcome.

Abiding means releasing results into God's hands. Trusting that He will shape, bless, or redirect the outcome as He sees fit.

Faith is not in the plan—it's in the Person guiding it. Let go, and walk with peace.

Prayer

Lord, I surrender the outcomes. Let me be faithful to walk with You and trust You with the results.

Prompt

What outcome are you holding onto tightly? Release it in prayer and ask God to lead your steps.

94

The Strength of Gentleness

Scripture

Galatians 5:23 - "The fruit of the Spirit is… gentleness…" (NIV)

Reflection

Gentleness is not weakness—it's strength under control.

Abiding shapes us into people who don't need to force, defend, or dominate. We reflect Jesus best when we carry His peace.

Allow your soul move softly today. The Spirit empowers you to lead with quiet strength.

Prayer

Holy Spirit, grow gentleness in me. Let my strength be clothed in softness and my presence bring peace.

Prompt

Is there a place where you've been operating with force rather than gentleness? Ask God to meet you there.

95

The Light Yoke

Scripture

Matthew 11:30 - "For my yoke is easy and my burden is light." (NIV)

Reflection

When your soul feels heavy, check the yoke you're carrying.

Jesus never burdens you with shame, striving, or hustle. His yoke is kind. His pace is grace.

Abiding means walking beside Him—not ahead, not behind. In rhythm. In peace.

Prayer

Jesus, teach me to walk in step with You. Teach me to bear only what comes from You, and lay down every burden that's not mine.

Prompt

Take inventory of your emotional load. What might Jesus be inviting you to lay down today so you can walk lighter?

96

Carried, Not Driven

Scripture

Isaiah 46:4 - "I have made you and I will carry you; I will sustain you and I will rescue you." (NIV)

Reflection

The world drives. God carries.

When you abide in Him, you're no longer pushed by pressure—you're lifted by love.

His strength doesn't demand more of you; it holds you in your weakness. Let yourself be carried today.

Prayer

God, carry me. In the places I feel weak, rushed, or overwhelmed—remind me I am held.

Prompt

Where are you trying to carry things on your own? Allow God lift that burden. Speak His promise from Isaiah 46:4 over your heart.

97

When Rest is Resistance

Scripture

Exodus 20:10 - "But the seventh day is a sabbath to the Lord your God. On it you shall not do any work…" (NIV)

Reflection

In a world obsessed with production, rest becomes a holy rebellion.

Sabbath is not laziness—it's resistance. A declaration that your worth is not tied to output.

Abiding includes stopping. Trusting. Honouring God by saying: I am enough because You are enough.

Prayer

Lord of the Sabbath, teach me to rest well. May my stillness be an offering, and my rest a witness to Your sufficiency.

Prompt

Plan a Sabbath moment this week—a window of time where you do nothing but enjoy God. How can you honour Him with your rest?

98

The Beauty of Still Waters

Scripture

Psalm 23:2 - "He leads me beside quiet waters, he refreshes my soul." (NIV)

Reflection

Stillness is not a stop—it's a restoration.

God leads you to quiet waters not to slow you down, but to refresh what life has drained.

Abiding means letting Him lead you to places of peace. Drink deeply. Rest freely. Allow your soul be restored.

Prayer

Good Shepherd, lead me again to still waters. Let my soul drink from Your peace and find new strength in Your presence.

Prompt

Picture the quiet waters of Psalm 23. What does your soul need to release so it can be refreshed there?

99

Unhurried Hope

Scripture

Romans 15:13 - "May the God of hope fill you with all joy and peace as you trust in him…" (NIV)

Reflection

Hope is not always loud. Sometimes it's quiet, steady, unhurried.

When you abide, your hope isn't based on what you see— it's rooted in who you know.

God fills you with peace not because everything is fixed, but because He is faithful. May hope rise slowly and surely today.

Prayer

God of hope, fill me. Let joy and peace overflow in me as I trust You—even in the waiting.

Prompt

What are you hoping for? Let your hope rest not in outcomes but in the God who holds them. Write a declaration of hope.

100

The Pace of Jesus

Scripture

Matthew 11:29 - "Take my yoke upon you and learn from me, for I am gentle and humble in heart..." (NIV)

Reflection

Jesus moved at the pace of love.

He was never rushed, yet always purposeful. He stopped for the one, noticed the unseen, and withdrew to be with the Father.

Abiding means learning His pace. A life shaped by gentleness, humility, and grace. Unhurried, but full of eternal purpose.

May your journey reflect the rhythm of Jesus—slow enough to notice, present enough to love, rooted enough to endure.

Prayer

Jesus, teach me Your pace. Let my life move with Your heart—unhurried, attentive, and full of grace.

Prompt

Look over the journey you've been on through these devotions. What has God shifted in you? What rhythm are you now choosing to live by?

Conclusion

This journey has not been about ticking boxes or finishing fast. It has been about walking slowly with God, learning to recognize His voice, His pace, and His peace.

You've taken 100 quiet steps toward stillness, intimacy, and rest. But this is not the finish line—it's the starting point of a new way of living.

As you go forward, carry the unhurried rhythms with you. Revisit devotions that spoke to you. Create sacred pauses in your day. Let your schedule reflect your surrender. And when the world tempts you to rush again, return to the One who walks slowly and speaks softly.

Jesus is still inviting you: "Come to Me, and I will give you rest."

Next Steps

1. Create a Rule of Life
Design a daily or weekly rhythm that includes silence, **Scripture**, prayer, and Sabbath. Keep it simple and sustainable.

2. Journal Your Journey
Use the journaling spaces in this devotional or a separate notebook to reflect on what God is showing you.

3. Revisit This Devotional
Don't feel bound to move on. Return to devotions that stirred you. Let them sink deeper over time.

4. Invite Others to Join You
Share this journey with friends, small groups, or church communities. The unhurried life is even richer when walked in companionship.

5. Practice Sabbath Regularly
Set aside a consistent time for soul rest–unhurried, unplugged, and undistracted.

6. Read **Scripture** Slowly
Meditate on one verse at a time. Linger long. Let the Word dwell richly within you.

7. Stay Near to the Shepherd
Above all, keep returning to Jesus. Stay close to the One who leads you beside still waters and restores your soul.

Closing Reflection
Living Unhurried

You've walked slowly through a hundred steps toward God's rest. But this isn't the end—it's the beginning of a new rhythm.

An unhurried life is not a lazy one. It is full of purpose, peace, and presence. It's rooted in love, paced by grace, and led by the Spirit. It doesn't mean you'll never be busy—but you'll no longer be bound by busyness. It doesn't mean you won't work hard—but now your work will flow from rest, not from restlessness.

The pace of Jesus is now your invitation. Continue walking with Him—slow, steady, surrendered. Let His peace govern your schedule. Let His voice lead your days. Let His rest shape your soul.

Unhurried is possible. Because Jesus walks with you.

Benediction

May you walk in step with the Spirit,
Work from a place of peace,
Wait without fear,
And worship in every pause.

May your soul find rest not just in moments, but in a lifestyle—
A life shaped by Jesus' pace, presence, and peace.

You are held.
You are loved.
And you are never alone on this unhurried journey.